THE BATTLE
OF BARKING CREEK

THE TRUE STORY OF THE FIRST FATALLITY OF WORLD WAR TWO WHICH HAPPENED ON THE THIRD DAY OF WAR, IN WHAT WE WOULD NOW CALL A FRIENDLY FIRE INCIDENT.

ALL THE ACTION TAKES PLACE IN THE COURTROOM OF FIGHTER COMMAND AT BENTLEY PRIORY.

CHARACTER BREAKDOWN.

JUDGE ADVOCATE STIRLING SCOTTISH 52

AIR VICE MARSHAL CALLAWAY RP 47

PILOT OFFICER FREEBORN YORKSHIRE 19

AIR COMMODORE BENNINGTON RP 46

SIR PATRICK HASTINGS RP 49

COURT USHER LONDON 37

SQUADRON LEADER DONALDSON RP 33

PILOT OFFFICER ROSE RP 21

FLIGHT LIEUTENANT MALAN SOUTH AFRICAN 29

FLYING OFFICER BYRNE IRISH 20

GROUP CAPTAIN LUCKING RP 35

EXTERIOR OF THE COURTROOM AT BENTLEY PRIORY.

Sir Patrick Hastings.

> Hello Freeborn, how are you.

Pilot Officer Freeborn

> Not too bad Sir, thank you for asking….I'm sorry Sir, actually I'm pretty bloody, I've never been so scared in all my life.

Sir Patrick Hastings.

> I'm sure you are Freeborn old chap but bear up, we'll get you through this…on a wing and a prayer old boy, on a wing and a prayer.

Pilot Officer Freeborn

> Yes Sir, thank you Sir.

INTERIOR OF THE COURTROOM AT BENTLEY PRIORY.

Court Usher.

> SILENCE IN COURT

Judge Advocate Sterling

> Orders by Air Vice Marshal Keith Park dated 23rd September 1939, London.

> The detail of officers mentioned below will assemble at RAF Headquarters, Bentley Priory on 17th October 1939 for the purpose of trying by General Courts Martial the accused persons named in the margin.

> Air Vice Marshal William Callaway is appointed President. Members are Air Commodore Charles Widdows, Group Captain Nigel Norman and Group Captain Leonard Horwood. Mr C L Sterling that is myself is appointed Judge Advocate, Air Commodore Gerald Bennington is appointed for the prosecution and Sir Patrick Hastings is acting for the defence.

Air VM Callaway

Pilot Officer Freeborn, do you object to being tried by me as President, or any of the other officers here before you.

Pilot Officer Freeborn

No Sir.

Judge Advocate Sterling

Have your rights under the rules of procedure been fully explained to you.

Pilot Officer Freeborn

Yes Sir.

Judge Advocate Sterling

Pilot Officer John Freeborn you are charged with insubordination, in that on the morning of 6th September you did cause the death of Pilot Officer Montague Hulton-Harrop by attacking his aircraft, shooting him in the head, directly contradicting an order to cease the attack. Are you guilty or not guilty of the charge against you.

Pilot Officer Freeborn

Not guilty.

Judge Advocate Sterling

Air Commodore Bennington, does the prosecution wish to make an opening address.

Air Com Bennington

Yes Sir. It is our case that on the morning of 6th September, only the third day after the declaration of war, that Pilot Officer Freeborn did shoot down and kill a fellow Officer… Pilot Officer Montague Hulton-Harrop.

It will be the case for the prosecution that this action was both reckless and foolhardy and in direct contradiction of an order to break off the attack

We will hear testimony that on that fateful morning of the 6th at 06-15 hours a searchlight battery reported enemy aircraft flying in the vicinity of West Mersea, Essex.

Sector operations at North Weald airfield received the report and they contacted headquarters to say they had scrambled a flight of six Hurricane fighters from 56 Squadron to find the enemy aircraft.

All this took place in the space of twelve minutes, a very impressive performance I think you'll agree.

Amazingly by this time twenty raids had been plotted by Radar and fifty hostile aircraft had also been reported by 11 Group.

All the information pointed to a mass attack and to this end fighters from 151 Squadron, North Weald were scrambled and shortly after aircraft of 74, 54 and 65 Squadrons were scrambled from Hornchurch to join the search for the enemy.

Two pilots from 56 Squadron belatedly jumped into two reserve aircraft and flew after their comrades, flying some 1000 feet below and half a mile behind.

They were attacked by Pilot Officer Freeborn and Flying Officer Byrne of 74 Squadron in direct contradiction of an

order from their Flight Commander to break off when it was realised they were in fact attacking friendly aircraft.

Judge Advocate Sterling

Thank you Air Commodore Bennington, now Sir Patrick Hastings opening statement for the defence.

Sir Patrick Hastings

Whilst not disagreeing greatly with the prosecution about the facts leading up to the fateful event where Pilot Officer Hulton-Harrop was shot down and killed.

I would like to point out that there was a great deal of confusion on the day, all of the sightings of enemy aircraft were later found to be false.

Serious errors were made that day but not by Pilot Officer Freeborn and Flying Officer Byrne who were both ordered to attack what they believed to be enemy aircraft and at no time did they receive an order to break off the attack.

Judge Advocate Sterling

Thank you Sir Patrick. Air Commodore Bennington do you wish to call your first witness.

Air Com Bennington

Yes Sir, I call Group Captain D F Lucking

Court Usher

Take the book in your right hand and repeat after me.

I swear by almighty God that the evidence I shall give before this court shall be the truth, the whole truth and nothing but the truth.

Group Captain Lucking

I swear by almighty God that the evidence I shall give before this court shall be the truth, the whole truth and nothing but the truth.

Air Com Bennington

Now, Group Captain you were Controller of Sector Operations at North Weald on the morning of the 6th and it was your responsibility to scramble the Squadrons at North Weald that day.

Group Captain Lucking

Yes Sir that's correct.

Air Com Bennington

Can you tell the court why so many aircraft were scrambled that day.

Group Captain Lucking

Well Sir, there weren't supposed to be so many, I only scrambled a Flight from 74 Squadron and was quite surprised to see the entire Squadron taking off.

Air Com Bennington

Why didn't you call them back when you realised too many aircraft were airborne.

Group Captain Lucking

The reports from HQ were constantly coming in suggesting there was a mass enemy attack so I took the decision that we would need all the aircraft we could muster to repel them.

Air Com Bennington

You say information was constantly coming in, so it's true to say the attack could have been called off at any time had it been deemed necessary.

Group Captain Lucking

Yes Sir, had we realised it was a false alarm we would have called off the attack immediately.

I'm afraid Sir, we were caught on the hop, it was only the third day after the declaration of war and we weren't ready.

Believe me Sir, it was one hell of a wake up call for all of us, I'm sorry, mistakes happen.

Air Com Bennington

Yes Group Captain, as you say mistakes happen but unfortunately when they result in the death of a fellow pilot some one has to be held responsible.

I have no further questions.

Judge Advocate Stirling

Sir Patrick.

Sir Patrick Hastings

Thank you. Now group Captain you said you were surprised to see the entire 74 Squadron take off, perhaps in retrospect it might have been better had you recalled them.

Group Captain Lucking

Yes Sir, it would but it's very easy to be wise after the event.

Sir Patrick Hastings

Group Captain, do you accept that it was your decision not to call aircraft to return to base that directly led to the death of Pilot Officer Hulton-Harrop.

Group Captain Lucking

NO SIR, I DIDN'T GIVE THE ORDER TO ATTACK.

Sir Patrick Hastings

No you didn't, but it was your decision to allow so many aircraft to take off that led to the confusion which caused the death of one of your airmen.

I have no further questions for this witness.

Judge Advocate Sterling

Air Commodore Bennington.

7

Air Com Bennington

Thank you, I call Squadron Leader Donaldson.

Court Usher

Squadron Leader Donaldson.

Air Com Bennington

Now you are the Squadron Leader of 151 Squadron based at North Weald.

Sqd Ldr Donaldson

Yes Sir, that is correct.

Air Com Bennington

And on the morning of 6th September I understand you were the second squadron to take off.

Sqd Ldr Donaldson

Yes Sir, I believe that is correct, we took off after 56 Squadron and climbed to our vectored height and went in search of the enemy.

There was a hell of a flap on that morning, there were aircraft from five different squadrons that had been scrambled.

Air Com Bennington

What happened later when you made contact with the enemy.

Sqd Ldr Donaldson

There was obviously a lot of confusion that morning, you have to remember it was only the third day of the war and we were all in a very heightened state of readiness, everyone was very jumpy that day.

Air Com Bennington

Yes, indeed Squadron Leader, but please just tell us what you saw when contact was made with the enemy.

Sqd Ldr Donaldson

I saw a very large group of aircraft which I assumed to be hostile until I visually confirmed that they were friendly Hurricanes.

I then saw two Spitfires turn in on two of the stragglers which I assumed to be Hurricanes and I yelled over the RT; DO NOT

RETALIATE, THEY ARE FRIENDLY, I called out three times at least, I don't know if anyone heard my transmission.

There was a Hell of a melee going on but neither of the Hurricanes fired back and in the end I saw both of them shot down, I couldn't believe it. I preyed to God they were alright, I mean they were our chaps.

I watched them go down and one didn't seem to be substantially damaged it just glided down in a left turn and hit the ground quite gently.

I later found out that that aircraft was piloted by Hulton-Harrop who had sadly been shot and killed.

Air Com Bennington

What did you do then.

Sqd Ldr Donaldson

I was extremely angry, HOW IN GODS NAME COULD WE HAVE SHOT DOWN TWO OF OUR OWN CHAPS.

I managed to get the wing re-formed and we headed back to North Weald, I couldn't believe how our controllers had vectored two of our wings into the same air space.

Air Com Bennington

Even so, that doesn't excuse the shooting down of innocent friendly aircraft.

Sqd Ldr Donaldson

No sir, it doesn't, but I'm afraid there was utter chaos going on that morning.

Air Com Bennington

Thank you Squadron Leader Donaldson, that will be all.

Judge Advocate Sterling

Sir Patrick, do you wish to cross examine this witness.

Sir Patrick Hastings

Yes Sir, I do. Now Squadron Leader you say there was a lot of confusion that morning and it was only the third day after the declaration of war.

Sqd Ldr Donaldson
>Yes Sir, that's correct.

Sir Patrick Hastings
>So at this time no-one had actually come into contact with enemy aircraft.

Sqd Ldr Donaldson
>Yes Sir, but we couldn't wait until we had the chance.

Sir Patrick Hastings
>What precautions had been taken with regard to aircraft recognition.

Sqd Ldr Donaldson
>Well Sir, we had aircraft recognition books which we used to study but it's obviously no substitute for the real thing.

Sir Patrick Hastings
>Yes Squadron Leader…. no substitute for the real thing. Thank you.

Judge Advocate Sterling
>Air Commodore, do you wish to re examine this witness.

Air Com Bennington
>No Sir, no further questions.

Judge Advocate Sterling
>Then please call your next witness.

Air Com Bennington
>I call Flight Lieutenant Adolph Malan.

Court Usher
>Flight Lieutenant Adolph Malan.

Air Com Bennington
>Flight Lieutenant Malan, I understand you were the Flight Commander of 74 Squadron.

Flight Lt Malan
>Yes Sir.

Air Com Bennington
> You were leader of Red Section, 74 Squadron and were the first aircraft to take off that morning.

Flight Lt Malan
> Yes Sir, I led Red Section and Yellow Section led by Flying Officer Byrne took off soon afterwards.

Air Com Bennington
> Who else was in Yellow Section.

Flight Lt Malan
> Pilot Officer Freeborn was flying as Yellow Two and Sergeant Pilot John Flinders was Yellow Three.

Air Com Bennington
> So you took off as Red Leader with Yellow Section close behind.

Flight Lt Malan
> Yes Sir, we climbed to our vectored height to the point where the enemy was supposed to be only to find it was a friendly Anson of Coastal Command.
>
> We were pretty miffed as we were hoping it was an enemy aircraft, so we joined the two flights together and went in search of Jerry.
>
> We caught sight of a wide Vic formation, which we thought were hostile but we were unable to get clear identification so we pressed on to attack the two aircraft which I thought were Messershmitt 109s which were flying behind and below.
>
> Yellow Section peeled off to attack the hostile 109s and at this point I realised they were friendly and called off the attack.

Air Com Bennington
> You definitely called off the attack.

Flt Lt Malan.
> Yes Sir, I definitely called off the attack.

Air Com Bennington
> Thank you Flight Lieutenant Malan, that will be all.

Judge Advocate Sterling
> Sir Patrick.

Sir Patrick Hastings

Thank you Sir.

Now Flight Lieutenant Malan it was you who ordered the attack on the two aircraft that later turned out to be friendly.

Flight Lt Malan

Yes Sir I did, but the second I realise they were friendly I called off the attack.

Sir Patrick Hastings

Indeed, then can you explain why we could find no-one from your squadron who could confirm your alleged RT message to break off the attack.

Flight Lieutenant Malan

I don't know Sir.

Sir Patrick Hastings

I suggest to you Flight Lieutenant that the reason no-one can corroborate your testimony is because YOU ARE A BARE FACED LIAR SIR.

Flt Lieutenant Malan

NO SIR, THAT'S NOT TRUE.

Judge Advocate Sterling

It's been a long morning and we're all getting a little weary, I think that unless Air Commodore Bennington wishes to re-examine this witness, this may be a good time to adjourn for lunch.

Air Com Bennington

I have no further questions Sir.

Judge Advocate Sterling

Excellent, then this court will adjourn for lunch and re-convene in one hours time.

ADJOURN FOR LUNCH.

Air V M Callaway

Welcome back everyone, may I remind you that I am Air Vice Marshal Callaway and I am the President of this Courts Martial.

I would like to say as we resume, that before luncheon some remarks were passed concerning the accuracy of the evidence of Flight Lieutenant Malan.

Whilst it may or may not be the case that Flight Lieutenant Malan was not telling the truth I wish to point out to all in this court that there are more gentlemanly ways to dispute evidence and I suggest we stick to them.

Judge Advocate Stirling

Thank you Air Vice Marshal, I'm sure we all agree with you and will be mindful of our language in the future.

I now call upon Air Commodore Bennington to call his next witness.

Air Com Bennington

Thank you Sir, I call Pilot Officer Frank Rose.

Court Usher

Call Pilot Officer Frank Rose.

Air Vice Mar Callaway

Pilot Officer Rose, I'm Air Vice Marshal Callaway and I'm the President of this Courts Martial.

I realise it's only six weeks since you were shot down and I just wanted to check you were physically up to this cross examination, we could adjourn if you're not up to it.

Pilot Officer Rose

Thank you sir, that's very kind of you, but I wasn't injured except for a few bruises when I crash landed.

Air Vice Mar Callaway

I'm glad to hear that Pilot Officer Rose, you had a very lucky escape.

Pilot Officer Rose
Yes Sir, very lucky, thank you.

Air Com Bennington
> Yes indeed, as the Air Vice Marshal says, a very lucky escape. Unfortunately your colleague Pilot Officer Hulton-Harrop was not to be as lucky as you were.

Pilot Officer Rose
> Yes Sir, that's correct…I would like to say, Sir that Hurrop was one of the nicest chaps you could have wished to meet and I miss him dearly.
> It's so sad that he bought it as he did, it's an awful mess… I would like Sir, if I could to extend my condolences to his family, I only recently met them but they will be in my heart forever.

Judge Advocate Stirling
> Indeed, I'm sure everyone here today joins with you in that… please continue Air Commodore.

Air Com Bennington
> Pilot Officer Rose, can you tell the court what happened on the fateful morning of the 6th.

Pilot Officer Rose
> Well Sir, it was a Wednesday and myself and Pilot Officer Hulton-Harrop were asleep as neither of us was on standby.
> I remember it was a Wednesday as we'd been really looking forward to a rest day for some time but we were woken by the damn bell and realised there was a flap on so we got out of bed to see what was happening, we were just expecting to see a flight take off.

Air Com Bennington
> A flight.

Pilot Officer Rose
> Yes Sir, a flight, just six aircraft.

Air Com Bennington
> And what did you see.

Pilot Officer Rose

Well Sir we stood and watched as the entire Squadron eventually take off.

Air Com Bennington

How many aircraft did you see take off.

Pilot Officer Rose

I can't be sure Sir, but the full Squadron was twenty four aircraft plus the others from 151 Squadron who shared the airfield with us.

By this time we assumed there must be a major flap on, so we joined in, we dragged our flying gear over our pyjamas and ran to our planes.

I remember shouting to Harrop; COME ON YOU BUGGER, RUN… that's the last thing I remember saying to him.

Air Com Bennington

So you and Pilot Officer Hulton-Harrop took off and attempted to catch up with your squadron.

Pilot Officer Rose

Yes Sir, we did, although as we had taken off later it took us longer to gain height and catch up… but we could see them in the distance.

Air Com Bennington

Then what happened.

Pilot Officer Rose

Well, I heard the RT crackle and Squadron Leader Donaldson shouting DO NOT RETALIATE, I didn't understand why, then seconds later I was being strafed by machine gun fire. I thought, MY GOD I'VE BEEN HIT, I'VE BEEN HIT…I didn't even see the bugger…I lost control of my aircraft and was plummeting towards the ground. I thought, DON'T LET IT END LIKE THIS, I'M TOO BLOODY YOUNG and I pulled with all my might on the damn stick and just managed to pull her level and belly flopped into a sugar beet field. I thought, BLIMEY THERE'LL BE HELL TO PAY FOR THIS, then I passed out.

Air Com Bennington

Yes, indeed Pilot Officer Rose and did you know what had happened to Pilot Officer Hulton-Harrop.

Pilot Officer Rose

No Sir, at that time I was just so pleased to come to and find I was alive and that I had been able to walk away from being shot down and surviving the belly flop.

I thought I'd been shot down by the enemy, I was astounded to find out later that I'd been shot down by one of ours.

Air Com Bennington

Thank you Pilot Office Rose, as you say, shot down by one of ours… a friendly aircraft, no further questions.

Judge Advocate Sterling

Sir Patrick do you wish to cross examine this witness.

Sir Patrick Hastings

Yes Sir, I do. Pilot Officer Rose you say your Squadron was the first to be scrambled that day and that the first aircraft took off at approximately 06-27.

Pilot Officer Rose

Yes Sir.

Sir Patrick Hastings

In your previous evidence you said you watched the entire squadron take off before you put on your flying gear and chased after your squadron.

Pilot Officer Rose

Yes Sir.

Sir Patrick Hastings

Do you know how long it was after your squadron had taken off before you became airborne.

Pilot Officer Rose

I couldn't say exactly sir, but it must have been about ten or fifteen minutes.

Sir Patrick Hastings

So you were some considerable distance behind your comrades when you took off.

Pilot Officer Rose

I wouldn't say considerable, we were at full throttle and full boost, we rung those planes out to catch up.

Sir Patrick Hastings

It has been stated that you and Pilot Officer

Hulton-Harrop were 1000 feet below and half a mile behind when you were both shot down.

Pilot Officer Rose

Yes Sir, I would say that's about right.

Sir Patrick Hastings

Did you at any time that morning consider that your actions were at all foolish.

Pilot Officer Rose

No Sir, not at all, there was an almighty flap on that day, if we'd have lost our aircraft because we left them on the ground that would have been foolish.

Sir Patrick Hastings

I'm suggesting to you that you were both shot down because you were in a place where no-one would have expected to find friendly aircraft and indeed the leading formation was totally unaware of your presence.

In fact the whole reason you and Pilot Officer Hulton-Harrop were shot down is because you placed yourselves in a position of danger where you were both seen as hostile aircraft.

Pilot Officer Rose

NO SIR, NO SIR, that's not true.

Sir Patrick Hastings

I have no further questions for this witness.

Judge Advocate Sterling

Do you wish to examine Air Commodore Bennington.

Air Com Bennington
Yes Sir, thank you.
Pilot Officer Rose can you tell the court what the weather conditions were that morning.

Pilot Officer Rose
Well Sir I have to say it was a beautiful summer morning, a little chilly but bright and clear.

Air Com Bennington
Bright and clear, you say, a beautiful summers morning.

Pilot Officer Rose
Yes Sir.

Air Com Bennington
It's hard, is it not Pilot Officer Rose, to understand therefore how anyone could have identified you as a hostile aircraft with such good visibility.

Pilot Officer Rose
Well, yes Sir.

Air Com Bennington
I think it's also fair to say that many people will agree with your opinion about getting your aircraft airborne and to a position of safety, but I think they will also agree that there can never be an excuse for shooting down a friendly aircraft whatever the circumstances.

Pilot Officer Rose
Yes Sir, no excuse.

Air Com Bennington
No further questions.

Judge Advocate Sterling
Then please call your next witness Sir Patrick.

Sir Patrick Hastings
I call Flying Officer Vincent Byrne.

Court Usher

Call Flying Officer Vincent Byrne.

Sir Patrick Hastings

Flying Officer Byrne, you were Yellow Leader on the morning of 6th September.

Flying Officer Byrne

Yes Sir.

Sir Patrick Hastings

We've heard of the events of that morning from other witnesses, can we hear your version.

Flying Officer Byrne

Well Sir, briefly it's simple, we took off and joined Red Section of 74 Squadron, we went looking for the enemy and found what we thought to be enemy aircraft.

There were two stragglers which we were ordered to attack which we did.

At no time during the attack did we have reason to question the order to attack nor did we receive any order to break off the attack.

It was sheer bad luck that the aircraft we attacked turned out to be friendly, GOD KNOWS I WISH IT WERE NOT TRUE, BUT IT WAS SHEER BAD LUCK, SIR.

Sir Patrick Hastings

You say you had no reason to question the order to attack.

Flying Officer Byrne

Yes Sir, we had no reason to question the order and if we had disobeyed there would have been Hell to pay.

We had no option we had to attack, had we not done so we would have been on a charge of insubordination.

Sir Patrick Hastings

Just to reiterate, at no time did you hear an order to call off the attack.

Flying Officer Byrne

Yes Sir, that's correct.

Sir Patrick Hastings

Thank you Flying Officer, no further questions.

Judge Advocate Sterling

Air Commodore Bennington do you wish to question this witness.

Air Com Bennington

Yes Sir I do. Flying Officer Byrne you said in your evidence you didn't hear any order to break off the attack.

Flying Officer Byrne

Yes Sir that's correct.

Air Com Bennington

Might I suggest to you Flying Officer that just because you didn't hear an RT message to break off doesn't mean one wasn't sent, there are any number of reasons why you may not have heard the message.

In the heat of what had now become battle perhaps your concentration was too fixed on the attack for you to notice.

Flying Officer Byrne

No Sir, if anything your senses become more heightened in a combat situation.

Air Com Bennington

Could it be that you switched radio channels during the attack.

Flying Officer Byrne

No Sir, we wouldn't have done that we were too focused on the attack.

Air Com Bennington

Too focused on the attack Flying Officer Byrne.

No further questions.

Judge Advocate Sterling

Sir Patrick do you wish to re-examine.

Sir Patrick Hastings

Yes Sir.

Flying Officer Byrne you just stated that your senses become more acute in a combat situation and that it is unlikely that you would have changed radio frequency during the battle.

You were all sufficiently alert to hear the order to attack, can you think of any other reason why you wouldn't have heard the message to break off.

Flying Officer Byrne
Yes Sir, no message was sent.

Sir Patrick Hastings
Thank you, no further questions.

Judge Advocate Sterling
Do you wish to call any further witnesses Sir Patrick.

Sir Patrick Hastings
Yes Sir I call my last witness Pilot Office John Freeborn.

Court Usher
Pilot Officer John Freeborn.

Sir Patrick Hastings
Pilot Officer Freeborn, on the morning of the 6th you were flying as Yellow Two of 74 Squadron.

Pilot Officer Freeborn
Yes Sir I took off behind Flying Officer Byrne who was Yellow Leader.

Sir Patrick Hastings
Please tell the court what happened up to the point where the unfortunate Hulton-Harrop was shot down and killed.

Pilot Officer Freeborn
Well Sir, we took off slightly behind Red Section as we had to wait for Paddy, that's Flying Officer Byrne to clear an engine misfire. We chased after Red Section to our vectored height and location only to find a friendly Anson of Coastal Command.
We stayed in a tight formation then suddenly we spotted the enemy and Flight Lieutenant Malan came over the RT shouting

TALLY HO, NUMBER ONE, ATTACK GO.

There was a hell of a lot of chaos going on , but we realised the aircraft we'd gone after were friendly so went after the two planes that were shadowing the main formation believing them to be hostile Messershmitt 109s. Flying Officer Byrne took one and I took the other, I fired a short burst and was surprised to see the aircraft plummet to the earth.

I never thought it would be that easy to shoot an aircraft down, but was obviously elated to have made my first kill of the war.

Sir Patrick Hastings

And then you flew back to base.

Pilot Officer Freeborn

Yes Sir, when I landed back at Hornchurch I could hear Sammy Samson our CO shouting, WHERE THE HELL IS MALAN, I WANT HIM HERE NOW.

But he'd done his usual bunk and gone home to his wife who was billeted off the airfield.

Myself and Flying Officer Bryne were both placed under close arrest and I was devastated when I was told the Messershmitt had in fact been a friendly aircraft.

We were both debriefed by the CO and that's all I can tell you Sir.

Sir Patrick Hastings

Thank you Pilot Officer Freeborn, I have just two further questions for you. Firstly can you confirm that you heard Flight Lieutenant Malan give the command Tally Ho, Number One, Attack Go.

Pilot Officer Freeborn

Yes Sir, everyone heard it.

Sir Patrick Hastings

And my second question for you, Pilot Officer is that at no time did you received the RT message to break off the attack.

Pilot Officer Freeborn

Yes Sir, at no time did we get the call to break off.

Sir Patrick Hastings
Thank you, no further questions.

Judge Advocate Sterling
Air Commodore Bennington.

Air Com Bennington
Thank you Sir.
I only have one question for this witness and that is , are you sure, and think carefully before you answer, are you sure that at no time you heard a RT message to break off the attack.

Pilot Officer Freeborn
Sir, I can tell you quite categorically that I have never before in my life been in a situation where I was so aware of my feelings.
My entire body was alive to a point I had no idea it could reach, my senses were so heightened I could have heard a pin drop in the cockpit let alone an RT message.

That's what combat is like Sir.

Judge Advocate Sterling
I assume that's all the questions you have for this witness Air Commodore.

Air Com Bennington
Yes Sir.

Judge Advocate Sterling
We have heard all the evidence and I now call upon Air Commodore Bennington to make his closing address.

Air Com Bennington
Thank you Sir.
The tragic death of Pilot officer Hulton-Harrop I believe, could have been avoided.
Were it not for the actions of Flying Officer Byrne and specifically Pilot Officer Freeborn, both young and inexperienced airmen I believe this tragedy would have been averted.
It is my contention that the irresponsible and gung ho actions of Pilot Officer Freeborn in particular caused the death of Pilot Officer Hulton-Harrop.

Whether or not you believe they were given the order to break off the attack, there can be no excuse for shooting down a friendly aircraft and for this reason alone I ask this court to find Pilot Officer Freeborn guilty.

Judge Advocate Sterling

Thank you Air Commodore, I now call upon Sir Patrick Hastings for his closing statement for the defence.

Sir Patrick Hastings

Thank you sir.

Young, inexperienced, yes they were, but all the airmen that day were young and inexperienced, it

was the third day of the war, no one had any experience of combat.

The whole day was peppered with unfortunate errors from the moment it started with the take off of so many aircraft; aircraft that could and perhaps should have been recalled.

The foolhardy but none the less understandable actions of Pilot Officer Hulton-Harrop and Pilot Officer Rose in chasing after their Squadron which led to them being identified as hostile aircraft.

The vectoring of two Wings of aircraft into the same air space was also a contributory factor which led to the order to attack being given.

Lastly and most importantly we could find no one who heard the order to break off the attack. The weight of evidence we believe gives this court no option but to find Pilot Officer Freeborn not guilty.

Judge Advocate Sterling

Thank you Sir Patrick. I would now ask that the court be cleared while Air Vice Marshal Callaway and the other members of this Courts Martial come to their decision.

Court Usher

Court rise.

THE COURT EMPTIES

EVERYONE RETURNS TO THE COURTROOM.

Judge Advocate Sterling

>Thank you for your patience everyone, Air Vice Marshal Callaway have you reached a verdict.

Air V M Callaway

>Yes Sir we have, but before we give our decision we would like on behalf of this court to offer our condolences to Pilot Officer Hulton-Harrops parents and family.
>
>This whole incident was full of unfortunate errors right from the start.
>
>Criticism can be levelled at the decision to allow too many aircraft to take off and the decision to vector two Wings into the same air space.
>
>We view the actions of Pilot Officer Hulton-Harrop and Pilot Officer Rose in taking off to follow their Squadron as foolish, but who here amongst us would not have done the same.
>
>Now to the evidence, and we feel the most crucial evidence of this Courts Martial, that of Flight Lieutenant Malan who ordered the attack on the unfortunate Pilot Officer Hulton-Harrop.
>
>We would criticise whole heartedly the evidence of this officer, the decision to attack was his and his alone and perhaps one made in haste, but under the circumstances understandable.
>
>What is not understandable and is the crucial point of this case is his evidence about the RT message to break off the attack.
>
>We believe that at no time was that message sent and we therefore find Pilot Officer John Freeborn, not guilty.